What's in this book

This book belongs to

T0351514

_____

献爱心 A helping hand

学习内容 Contents

沟通 Communication

问问某人是谁
Ask who or whom someone is

询问及回答谁是物品主人
Ask and respond to questions about personal belongings

生词 New words

★	是	to be
★	谁	who, whom
★	这	this
★	那	that
★	男孩	boy
★	女孩	girl
	铅笔	pencil
	本子	notebook
	足球	football

他是谁?
Who is he?

这是谁的铅笔?
Whose pencil is this?

那是不是你的铅笔?
Is that your pencil?

那是/不是我的铅笔。
That is/is not my pencil.

跨学科学习 Project

将物品分类以便回收,利用
废纸制作手工
Sort items for recycling and
make crafts from scrap paper

文化 Cultures

中国古代足球
Ancient Chinese football

Get ready

1 What is the poster about?

2 Do you have similar posters in your school?

3 What would you do?

故事大意：

学校举办募捐活动，同学们踊跃参与，带了很多东西回学校。最后，大家看着满满一箱的文具和玩具，疑惑捐助的物品是否能够帮助到他人。

询问某人是谁时，我们说"你（们）/他（们）/她（们）是谁？"其中"谁"在询问人物时表示疑问。用"我（们）/他（们）/她（们）是……"来回答。

tā shì shéi

他是谁？

询问谁是物品的主人时，我们说"这/那是谁的？"或"……是谁的？"可用"这/那是我（们）/你（们）/他（们）/她（们）的。"或"……是我（们）/你（们）/他（们）/她（们）的。"来回答。

zhè shì shéi de

这是谁的？

他是谁？ 这是谁的铅笔？ 谁的本子？

参考问题和答案：

1 Who do you think is the boy on the poster? (He represents the children who need help.)

2 What are Ms Wu and the schoolmates doing? (The schoolmates are gathering donations. Ms Wu is asking about whose things these are.)

zhè shì wǒ de

这是我的。

时间、地点或事物跟自己（说话人）距离较近时，我们说"这"。

nà shì tā de

那是他的。

时间、地点或事物跟自己（说话人）距离较远时，我们说"那"。

他是……这是我的铅笔。
那是他的本子。

参考问题和答案：

1　Whose pencils are these? (These are Ling Ling's pencils.)

2　Whose notebook is that? (That is Hao Hao's notebook.)

那是谁的足球？

参考问题和答案：

What is Ms Wu asking about? (She is asking whose footballs those are.)

那是男孩的足球。那是我们的！

参考问题和答案：

1 Who answered the question? What does he/she say? (Ethan answered the question and he says, 'That football is ours.')
2 Which football is the boys'? (The blue one is the boys'.)

nǚ hái
女孩

那是女孩的足球。那不是我们的！

参考问题和答案：
What is Ethan saying? (He is saying that the pink ball is the girls'.)

我们的东西，能帮助他人吗？

参考问题和答案：

1　How do the schoolmates look? (They look confused. They are thinking hard.)

2　What do you think they are thinking about? (They are wondering whether these donations can help others.)

Let's think

1 What did the children donate? Tick the boxes and write the correct letters in the blanks.

提醒学生回忆故事，观察第4至9页。同时要将人物与其捐赠的物品配对。

这是我的 __a__。

这是我们的 __c__。

这是我的 __e__。

这是我的 __d__。

参考答案：
Pencils and notebooks are necessary for learning. Dolls and footballs are good for playing and having fun.

2 How can these items help the children in need? Discuss with your friend.

老师可以提醒学生，捐赠时应该了解他人需要什么，不要捐赠无用、破旧和不卫生的物品。

New words

1 Learn the new words.

女孩　本子　足球　男孩　铅笔　谁　这　是　那

2 Complete the sentences. Write the letters.

a 这　b 那　c 女孩　d 男孩　e 不　f 谁

1

__b__ 是 __d__
的足球。

2

__a__ 是 __c__
的足球吗？

3

这是__f__
的本子？

4

这 __e__ 是
我的铅笔。

提醒学生注意手所指的物品远近。并总结离说话人近的用"这"，远的用"那"。

11

听听说说 Listen and say

第一题录音稿：
1 玲玲：浩浩，这是谁的
浩浩：这是我的。
2 这不是弟弟的果汁。这
姐姐的果汁。
3 这是女孩的足球。那是
孩的足球。

🎧 03 **1** Listen and circle the correct pictures.

1

2

🎧 04 **2** Look at the pictures. Listen to

① 这是谁的铅笔？

那不是我的铅笔，那是哥哥的。

3

③ 那不是我们的铅笔。

第二题参考问题和答案：

1 Whose pencils are these? Answer in Chinese. (这是伊森/艾文爸爸的铅笔。)

2 Have you ever lost something at home? (Yes, I lost my Chinese book once and my mum found it the next day.)

提醒学生观察左边第二题的小漫画，根据故事情节进行排序。

ry and say.

3 Number the pictures in order. Role-play with your friends.

Task

Role-play with your friends. Find the owners of the lost items.

老师先带领学生复习对话句式，再由学生角色扮演练习对话。
还可以将铅笔替换成图中或教室里的其他物品。

Song

歌词动作参考：让学生唱到"是"时点头，"不是"时摇头，"谁的"时望向左右两边的同学，"我的"时用手指向自己，"你的"时两个同学互相指向对方。

 Listen and sing.

这是谁的铅笔？

那是谁的本子？

铅笔是我的，

本子是他的。

铅笔不是他的，

本子不是你的，

这是我的，你的呢？

课堂用语 Classroom language

别叫。
Don't shout.

别说话。
Don't talk.

15

1 Trace the strokes to complete the characters. 提醒学生先回忆笔画"横折"的写法，再进行描写笔画。

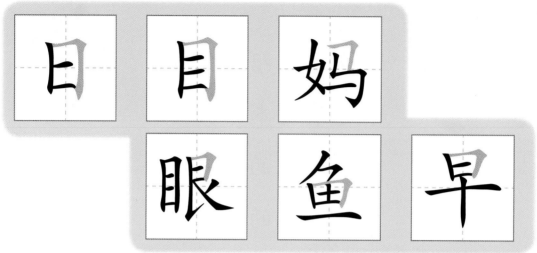

日 目 妈
眼 鱼 早

2 Learn the component. Circle 田 in the characters.

田 鱼 男 画 由

3 How many 田 can you find? Circle the correct answer.

a 十三
a 九
ⓒ 十
d 五

四个小方块即一个"田"字，老师提醒学生要仔细数，不要漏掉重叠部分的方块。

4 Trace and write the character.

提醒学生"田"中间的竖和"力"的撇
不连在一起。

汉字小常识 Did you know?

Two or more components combined can give a clue to the meaning of a character.

田 (field) and 力 (strength) combined mean 'man'/'men'. This is because in ancient China, men worked in the fields.

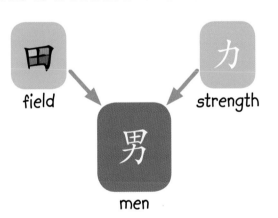

Can you guess the meaning of the character 明?

The character 明 means 'bright'. Brightness comes from the sunlight and the moonlight.

Cultures

蹴鞠是现代足球运动的起源。这是一种以脚击球的运动，相传本为军训之用，后来演变为游戏。"蹴"即"踢"，"鞠"即"球"。

1 Learn about ancient Chinese football.

Cuju (蹴鞠), a team ball game, was popular in ancient China.

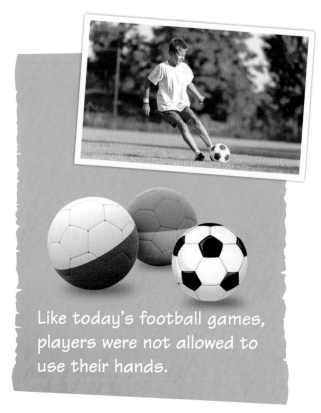

Like today's football games, players were not allowed to use their hands.

2 Circle the Chinese football in the old paintings.

提醒学生留意图中的人物包括女性和男性，同时蹴鞠既可作为娱乐又是一种专业运动。

老师和学生一起讨论废旧物品及垃圾的回收分类问题。

1 玩具熊、帽子和足球是可以继续使用的物品，应放入捐赠箱去帮助有需要的人。

2 左侧第一个垃圾桶是放一些不可回收的垃圾，故苹果芯和厨房锡纸应放在这里。

3 剩下的四个垃圾桶都是收纳可回收利用的废弃物，依次回收塑料制品、玻璃制品、废纸和金属类制品。

4 最后老师提醒学生回忆生活中的经历，再将垃圾桶涂上合适的颜色。作为参考，广泛规定的是可回收物的桶一般为蓝色，不可回收物的桶一般为黄色。

Project

1 Where should the items go? Match them to the right places.

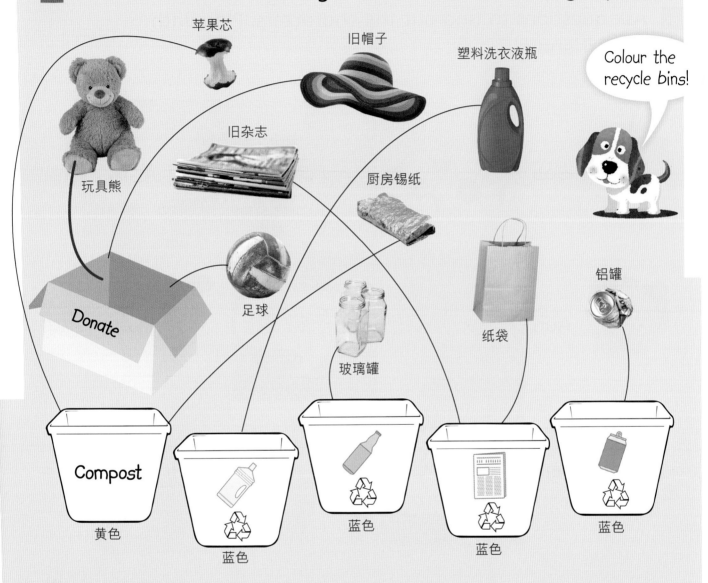

2 Do not throw away used paper, make art!

准备好平时使用后多余的红、绿卡纸各一张，以及若干个废弃卷筒。

先将绿色卡纸剪成树的形状，再贴上从红色卡纸剪下的条状装饰物，并用彩笔画一些图案做点缀。

将废弃卷筒涂成棕色，再把上一步完成的圣诞树贴到卷筒上即可。

游戏方法：

九宫格左侧是三个小朋友，头像右侧那一行是有关他们年龄和物品的描述。学生 2–3 人一组，其中一人自己在心中选定人物，其他人向其进行提问，并根据得到的回答来确定是哪一个小朋友。

建议句式："他/她是不是……""他/她几岁？" "他/她有没有……"

1 Ask questions to find out the characters. Play with your friend.

评核方法：

学生两人一组，互相考察评价表内单词和句子的听说读写。交际沟通部分由老师朗读要求，学生再互相对话。
如果达到了某项技能要求，则用色笔将星星或小辣椒涂色。

2 Work with your friend. Colour the stars and the chillies.

Words			
是	☆	☆	🌶
谁	☆	☆	🌶
这	☆	☆	🌶
那	☆	☆	🌶
男孩	☆	☆	🌶
女孩	☆	☆	🌶
铅笔	☆	🌶	🌶
本子	☆	🌶	🌶
足球	☆	🌶	🌶

Sentences			
这是谁的本子？	☆	🌶	🌶
那是不是你的铅笔？	☆	🌶	🌶
那是/不是我的铅笔。	☆	🌶	🌶

Ask who or whom someone is	☆
Ask and respond to questions about personal belongings	☆

3 What does your teacher say?

评核建议：

根据学生课堂表现，分别给予"太棒了！
(Excellent!)"、"不错！(Good!)"或"继续努力！
(Work harder!)"的评价，再让学生圈出左侧对
应的表情，以记录自己的学习情况。

My teacher says ...

Words I remember

是	shì	to be
谁	shéi	who, whom
这	zhè	this
那	nà	that
男孩	nán hái	boy
女孩	nǚ hái	girl
铅笔	qiān bǐ	pencil
本子	běn zi	notebook
足球	zú qiú	football

Other words

献	xiàn	to dedicate
爱心	ài xīn	love
我们	wǒ men	we, us
他们	tā men	they, them
东西	dōng xi	thing
帮助	bāng zhù	to help
他人	tā rén	other people
吗	ma	(question word)

OXFORD
UNIVERSITY PRESS

Oxford University Press is a department of the University of Oxford.
It furthers the University's objective of excellence in research, scholarship,
and education by publishing worldwide. Oxford is a registered trade mark of
Oxford University Press in the UK and in certain other countries

Published in Hong Kong by
Oxford University Press (China) Limited
39th Floor, One Kowloon, 1 Wang Yuen Street, Kowloon Bay,
Hong Kong

© Oxford University Press (China) Limited 2017

The moral rights of the author have been asserted

First Edition published in 2017

All rights reserved. No part of this publication may be reproduced, stored in a
retrieval system, or transmitted, in any form or by any means, without the prior
permission in writing of Oxford University Press (China) Limited, or as expressly
permitted by law, by licence, or under terms agreed with the appropriate
reprographics rights organization. Enquiries concerning reproduction outside
the scope of the above should be sent to the Rights Department, Oxford
University Press (China) Limited, at the address above

You must not circulate this work in any other form
and you must impose this same condition on any acquirer

Illustrated by Anne Lee and Wildman

Photographs for reproduction permitted by Dreamstime.com

China National Publications Import & Export (Group) Corporation is an authorized distributor of
Oxford Elementary Chinese.

Please contact content@cnpiec.com.cn or 86-10-65856782

ISBN: 978-0-19-082144-9

10 9 8 7 6 5 4 3 2

Teacher's Edition
ISBN: 978-0-19-082156-2

10 9 8 7 6 5 4 3 2